30/2074H

5

The Amazing Music Activities Book

Ideas and Exercises for Exploring:

- ♪ Music Basics
- ♪ Ear Training
- ♪ Music Styles
- ♪ Famous Composers

by Janet Vogt

Music Engraving: Linda Taylor
Type and Cover Design: Patti Jeffers

© 2006 Heritage Music Press, a division of The Lorenz Corporation, and its licensors. All rights reserved.
Printed in the United States of America
ISBN: 0-89328-225-1

HMP
HERITAGE MUSIC PRESS
A Division of The Lorenz Corporation
Box 802 / Dayton, OH 45401-0802
www.lorenz.com

Foreword

A friend of mine (a classroom teacher for many years) once said something to me that changed the way I teach. He said, "Every moment is a teachable moment." I stopped and considered how teaching can become a laundry list of checking the previous assignment, correcting the assignment, quickly explaining the requirements of the next assignment and getting caught up in details instead of the thrill of sharing and exploring new ideas together. I have made it my goal since then to try to never miss those moments. In this book, you will find many pencil-to-paper activities that I hope give you the opportunity to share music concepts in a fresh and new way, maybe even with a giggle or two.

I have also found (as I'm sure you have, too) that music is meant to be listened to and experienced, and not just discussed in the abstract. That is why in this book, you'll find real ear training exercises that give your young students the confidence and knowledge to identify what they hear – from the simplest concepts to beginning dictation. I remember when I was pursuing my Masters in Music Theory at the Cincinnati Conservatory, I was a teaching assistant and, of course, routinely had to give ear training exams. My class, which consisted of many voice majors or freshman with limited music reading skills, would sweat their way through melodic dictation in particular. They would get hung up on a rhythm or a part of the melody and the rest of the dictation would fall apart, so I devised a way for them to isolate the rhythmic and melodic portions. I have featured that same system in this book and I hope you and your students find it very helpful. I also know from all those music history classes that the teachers could talk about the elegance of the Classical Period, but when they walked over to the record player (yes, a record player in my time) and put on a recording, then and only then did the concept really came alive. For that reason, with each composer biography, I have created brief orchestral and chamber music reductions of some of their most recognizable themes to help their music come alive to each of your students.

From *Tee-Shirt Tunes* to *Two-Step Dictations* to a brief look at composers' lives and their music, I hope this book delights your students and brings to you many "teachable moments."

Janet Vogt

Contents

Rainbows 'n' Butterflies

Can you make a rainbow out of this musical staff?
Color the F space green. Color the A space yellow.
Color the C space blue. Color the E space red.

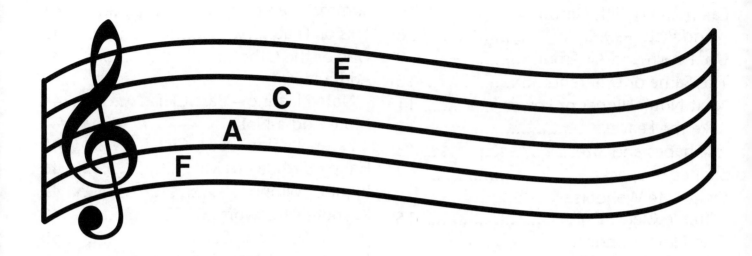

Butterfly Melody

The butterflies are landing on the musical staff. Find the butterfly that has landed on the F space and write the letter F on that butterfly. Find the butterfly that has landed on the A space and write an A on that butterfly. Find the butterfly that has landed on the C space and write a C on that butterfly. Find the butterfly that has landed on the E space and write an E on that butterfly. Then color each of your butterflies.

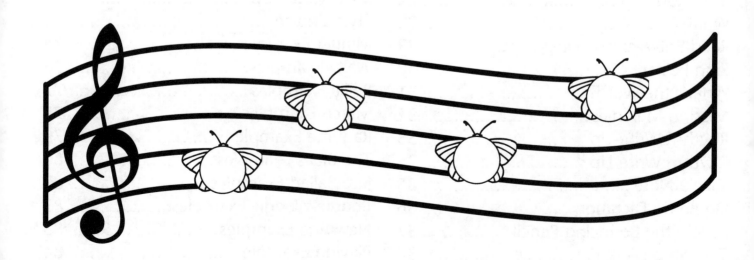

Laundry Day

Time to hang up all those freshly washed clothes on the musical staff below. But first, turn each line into a colorful line to hang those clothes. Trace the E line with a red crayon. Trace the G line with a blue crayon. Trace the B line with a yellow crayon. Trace the D line with a green crayon, and trace the F line with a purple crayon.

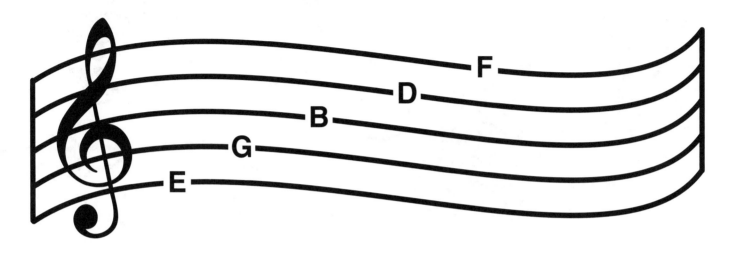

Tee Shirt Tune

Time to hang up the shirts. Write an E on the shirt that is hanging on the E line, write a G on the shirt that is hanging on the G line, write a B on the shirt that is hanging on the B line, write a D on the shirt that is hanging on the D line, and write an F on the shirt that is hanging on the F line. Then color each of your tee shirts.

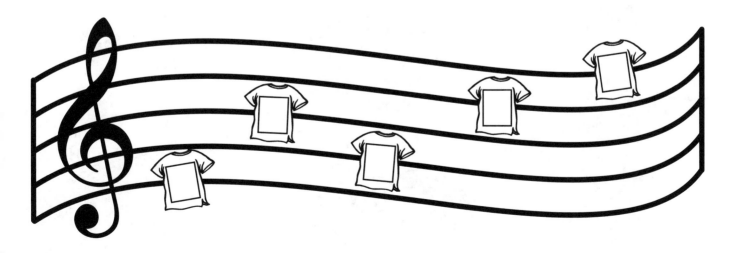

30/2074H-5

Imagine This

Can you imagine the sound that each picture below is making? Is it *f* (*forte*, loud) or *p* (*piano*, soft)? Add an *f* or *p* to each thought balloon below to indicate the sound (loud or soft) of each picture.

purrrr . . .

Tweet

Roar!

Honk! Honk!

Either Or

Your teacher will play several musical examples for you. They will either be *forte* (loud) or *piano* (soft), notes going up (↑) or notes going down (↓), low sounds or high sounds, legato (smooth and connected notes) or staccato (short and disconnected notes). Circle the correct answer in each square.

1. *forte (f)* or *piano (p)*	**2.** High Sounds or Low Sounds	**3.** Notes Going Up ↑ or Notes Going Down ↓
4. Legato or Staccato	**5.** *forte (f)* or *piano (p)*	**6.** Notes Going Up ↑ or Notes Going Down ↓
7. High Sounds or Low Sounds	**8.** Legato or Staccato	**9.** Notes Going Up ↑ or Notes Going Down ↓

See page 84 for Teacher's Examples.

30/2074H-7

Ear Training with Gestures and Pictures

Listening for Note Direction

In this exercise, your students will listen to the following melody, *Dance of the Leaves,* and determine if the melody notes travel up, down, wiggle around, or stay the same. Have the students stand with arms extended in front of them like the wind, ready to push and pull at the falling leaves. As the melody notes flutter down, the students should move their arms and hands in the same direction as the melody. If the melody begins to sweep up, the students should gesture with an upward motion. Students should continue to "conduct" the melody, mimicking the note direction with the appropriate motion of their arms and hands.

Dance of the Leaves

Play the melody again and have your students draw and chart the shape of the melody with simple directional lines that follow the shape of the tune. For example:

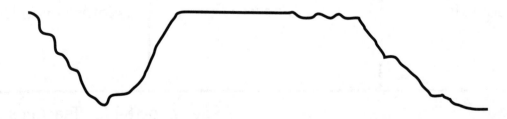

Up, Down and All Around

Notes can move up (↑) , notes can move down (↓) or notes can stay the same and repeat (→). As your teacher plays several musical examples for you, draw an up arrow in the box if the notes move up, draw a down arrow if the notes move down or draw a sideways arrow if the notes repeat and stay the same.

1.	2.	3.
4.	5.	6.
7.	8.	9.

See page 84 for Teacher's Examples.

30/2074H-9

The Same or Different?

Your teacher will play two short musical examples in a row. Circle the "same" if each musical example is identical. Circle "different" if the examples are not the same.

1. Same or Different	**2.** Same or Different	**3.** Same or Different
4. Same or Different	**5.** Same or Different	**6.** Same or Different
7. Same or Different	**8.** Same or Different	**9.** Same or Different

See page 85 for Teacher's Examples.

Next Note: Higher or Lower

Your teacher will play several 2-note musical examples for you. Listen closely and determine whether the second note is higher or lower than the first note. Circle "higher" if the second note is higher than the first note. Circle "lower" if the second note is lower than the first note.

1.	2.	3.
Higher or Lower	Higher or Lower	Higher or Lower
4.	5.	6.
Higher or Lower	Higher or Lower	Higher or Lower
7.	8.	9.
Higher or Lower	Higher or Lower	Higher or Lower

See page 85 for Teacher's Examples.

30/2074H-11

Rake the Leaves

There are four kinds of notes:

(♩) Quarter Note = 1 beat   (♪) Half Note = 2 beats

(♩.) Dotted Half Note = 3 beats   (o) Whole Note = 4 beats

All the leaves are falling and it's time to rake them up. Draw a line to connect all the quarter note leaves to the trash can; all the half note leaves to the basket; all the dotted half note leaves to the wheelbarrow; and all the whole note leaves to the lawn bag.

All Shapes and Sizes

Any note, like C, D, or E, can be a quarter note (♩), half note (♩), dotted half note (♩.) or whole note (o).

For example:

C Quarter Note
1 beat

C Half Note
2 beats

C Dotted Half Note
3 beats

C Whole Note
4 beats

Draw a line to connect the quarter note C to each C, the quarter note D to each D, and the quarter note E to each E.

1.

2.

3.

13

30/2074H-13

5 Lines, 4 Spaces

The music staff has 5 lines and 4 spaces:

Notes may be line notes or space notes:

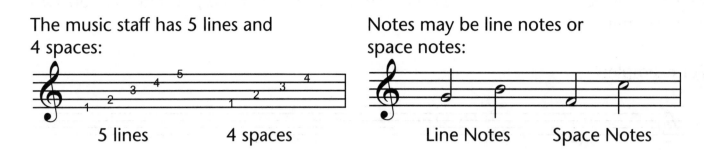

5 lines   4 spaces   Line Notes   Space Notes

Label each note below as a line note (L) or a space note (S).

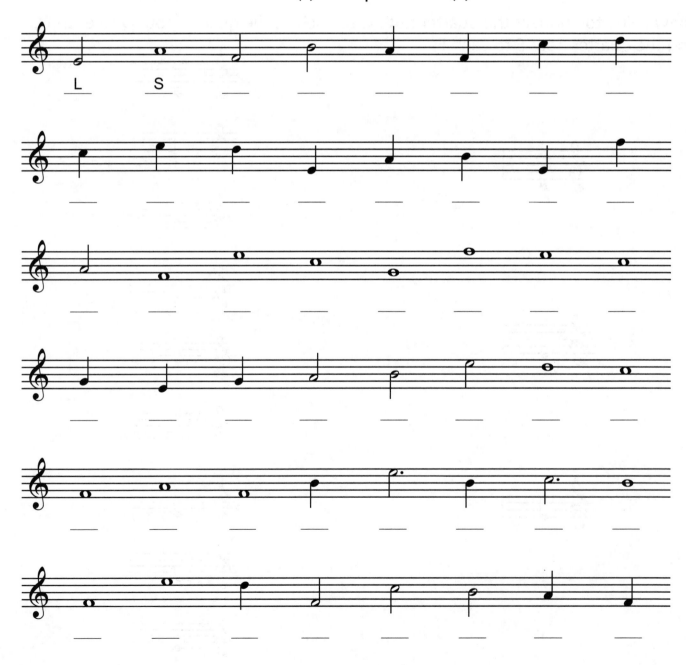

One-Note Wonders: Treble Clef C-D-E-F-G

Middle C hangs slightly below the staff. It has a short line (ledger line) running through it.

D hugs the bottom line of the staff.

E is a line note with the first line of the staff running through it.

F is a space note. It sits between the first two lines of the staff.

G is a line note with the second line of the staff running through it.

Circle only the C notes.

Circle only the D notes.

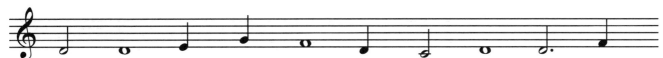

Circle only the E notes.

Circle only the F notes.

Circle only the G notes.

30/2074H-15

One-Note Wonders: Bass Clef C-D-E-F-G

C is a space note that sits between the second and third line on the staff.

D is a line note with the third or middle line of the staff running through it.

E is a space note that sits between the third and fourth line of the staff.

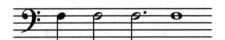

F is a line note with the fourth line of the staff running through it.

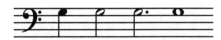

G is a space note that sits between the fourth and fifth line of the staff.

Circle only the C notes.

Circle only the D notes.

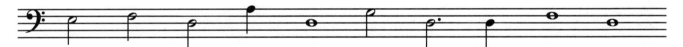

Circle only the E notes.

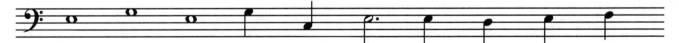

Circle only the F notes.

Circle only the G notes.

Building Dynamics

Dynamic markings indicate the "louds" and "softs" in music. From softest to loudest, they are:

pp	**p**	**mp**	**mf**	**f**	**ff**
pianissimo, very soft	*piano,* soft	*mezzo piano,* medium soft	*mezzo forte,* medium loud	*forte,* loud	*fortissimo,* very loud

Trace each dynamic marking below:

pp   p   mp   mf   f   ff   f

Build the picture below by connecting the dynamic markings from the softest to the loudest.

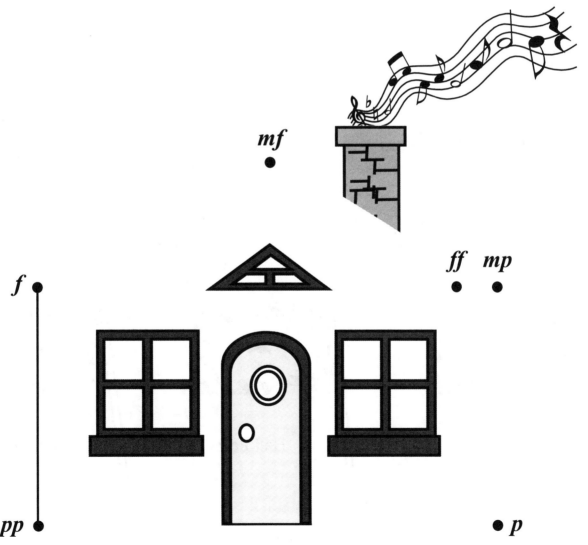

30/2074H-17

Race to the Finish

In music, rests indicate silence. Whenever you see a rest, think "shhhhhh."

Quarter Rest 𝄽
Rest for one beat.

Half Rest ▬
Rest for two beats
(looks like a hat).

Whole Rest ▬
Rest for a whole
measure.

Draw a line to drive each race car to the finish line flag it matches. Then count up how many cars passed each flag. Who won the race with the most number of rests?

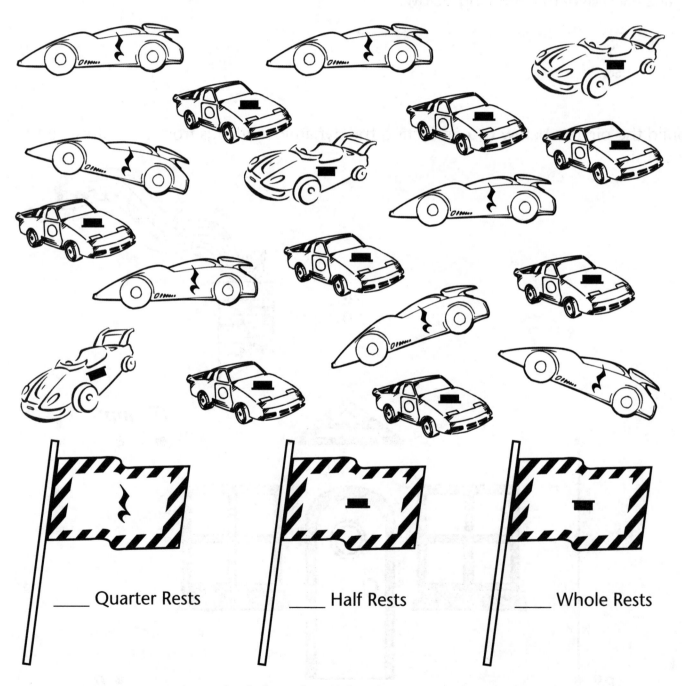

_____ Quarter Rests   _____ Half Rests   _____ Whole Rests

And the winner is _____!

Sign of the Times

Below are common musical signs and symbols.

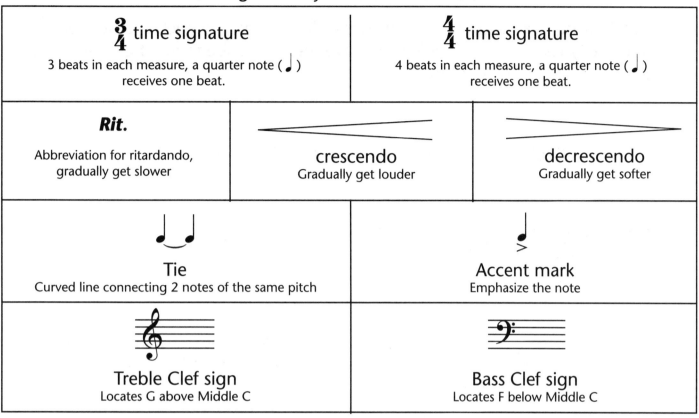

¾ time signature 3 beats in each measure, a quarter note (♩) receives one beat.	**⁴⁄₄ time signature** 4 beats in each measure, a quarter note (♩) receives one beat.

Rit. Abbreviation for ritardando, gradually get slower	**crescendo** Gradually get louder	**decrescendo** Gradually get softer

Tie Curved line connecting 2 notes of the same pitch	**Accent mark** Emphasize the note
Treble Clef sign Locates G above Middle C	**Bass Clef sign** Locates F below Middle C

Draw a line to connect each billboard to the musical signs or symbols they are advertising.

30/2074H-19

Ear Training with Singing
Matching Pitches and Determining Note Direction

Play the following examples for your students. Have them sing each example back to you using the lyrics "Trick or Treat". Then have them describe to you how the notes moved within each melodic fragment.

Example (Play, then sing with the class.)	Note Direction
Trick or Treat!	Notes repeat.
Trick or Treat!	Notes move up by step, then back down by step.
Trick or Treat!	Notes move down by step, then back up by step.
Trick or Treat!	Notes skip up, then skip down.
Trick or Treat!	Notes skip down, then skip up.

Create other short patterns for your students to sing back to you and describe. For fun, use the names of your students for the lyrics.

Next Note: Step or Skip

Your teachers will play several 2-note examples for you. Listen closely to determine whether the second note is a step away from the first note or a skip away from the first note. Hint: Here is a good way to help you make your choice. If the two notes sound like they can be the beginning of a scale, they are a step apart. If the two notes sound like they can begin to outline a three-note chord or a triad, then they are a skip apart.

For Example:

Sounds like Do Re Mi Fa Sol
(the beginning of a scale)

Sounds like Do Mi Sol
(part of a three-note chord)

Circle "Step" or "Skip" as your teacher plays each example.

1.	2.	3.
Step or Skip	Step or Skip	Step or Skip
4.	**5.**	**6.**
Step or Skip	Step or Skip	Step or Skip
7.	**8.**	**9.**
Step or Skip	Step or Skip	Step or Skip

See page 85 for Teacher's Examples.

30/2074H-21

Question, Please

Match each musical symbol with its question.

1. _____ *f*

2. _____ **rit.**

3. _____ ———————

4. _____ **mp**

5. _____ ♩♩

6. _____ **mf**

7. _____ ♩

8. _____ 𝄾

9. _____ ♩.

10. _____ *p*

11. _____ ———————

12. _____ ♩

13. _____ ▬

14. _____ ▬

15. _____ **ff**

16. _____ **pp**

A. *What is the symbol for mezzo piano?*

B. *What is the symbol for a half rest?*

C. *What is the symbol for a tie?*

D. *What is the symbol for crescendo?*

E. *What is the symbol for fortissimo?*

F. *What is the symbol for decrescendo?*

G. *What is the symbol for piano?*

H. *Which note is a quarter note?*

I. *What is the symbol for ritardando?*

J. *What is the symbol for forte?*

K. *Which note is a dotted half note?*

L. *What is the symbol for a whole rest?*

M. *What is the symbol for pianissimo?*

N. *What is the symbol for mezzo forte?*

O. *What is the symbol for a quarter rest?*

P. *Which note is a half note?*

I Spy a Tie (and other Cool Stuff)

Locate and circle each musical symbol(s) in the picture below. Put a checkmark beside each symbol search that you complete.

_____ A tie

_____ 5 treble clef signs

_____ 4 bass clef signs

_____ 2 *piano* (*p*) signs

_____ 1 *mezzo piano* (*mp*) sign

_____ 2 *mezzo forte* (*mf*) signs

_____ 1 *forte* (*f*) sign

_____ 8 half notes

_____ 1 dotted half note

_____ 4 quarter rests

_____ 1 half rest

_____ 2 whole rests

_____ 2 $\frac{3}{4}$ time signatures

_____ 1 $\frac{4}{4}$ time signature

_____ 2 turtles

23

Riddles 'n' More

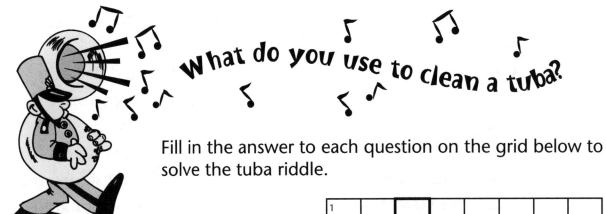

Fill in the answer to each question on the grid below to solve the tuba riddle.

1. ♩ _____ note.

2. ♪ eighth _____.

3. "Omm-pah" goes the _____.

4. A ___ CDEFG, the musical alphabet.

5. ▬ _____ rest.

6. Abbreviation for ritardando _____.

7. 𝅗 _____ note.

8. *f* (loud) or _____.

9. ♩‿♩ curved line or _____.

10. 𝅗𝅥 _____ note.

11. *p* (soft) or _____.

12. 𝅘𝅥 _____ mark.
    >

13. 𝄽 quarter _____.

14. 𝅗𝅥. _____ half note.

15. *mp* _____ piano.

A. *What is a rabbit's favorite musical style?*

B. *What is the most musical part of the turkey?*

C. *What do you call a musical automobile?*

C. Cartoon   B. The drumstick   A. Hip-Hop

Flag Day

Study the note chart, then name each note in the flags below.

30/2074H-25

Picture This

Each picture below can be spelled with notes from the musical alphabet. Study the note chart below, then using whole notes, spell each note on the musical staff. Write the name of each note on the blank lines.

Note Chart

C D E F G A B

1.

2.

3.

4.

5.

6.

7. Honest

8.

9.

It All Adds Up

Music is just like math. In $\frac{4}{4}$ time, the beats in each measure must always add up to 4. In $\frac{3}{4}$ time, the beats in each measure must always add up to 3.

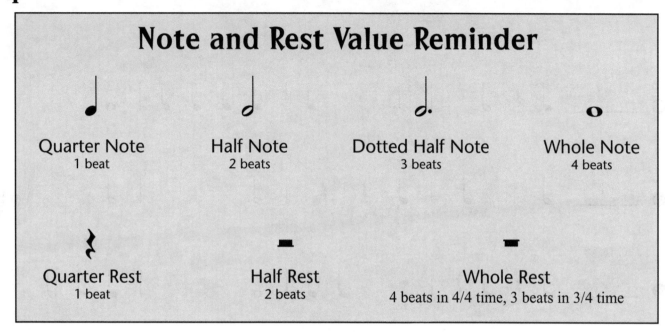

Add notes or rests to the incomplete measures in each example below. Make sure each measure adds up to the correct number of beats.

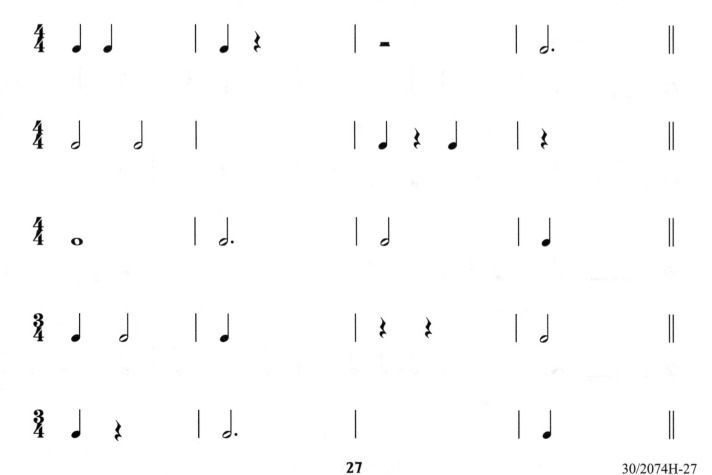

What Time Is It?

Study each example below, then write in the missing time signature ($\frac{3}{4}$ or $\frac{4}{4}$) at the beginning of each example.

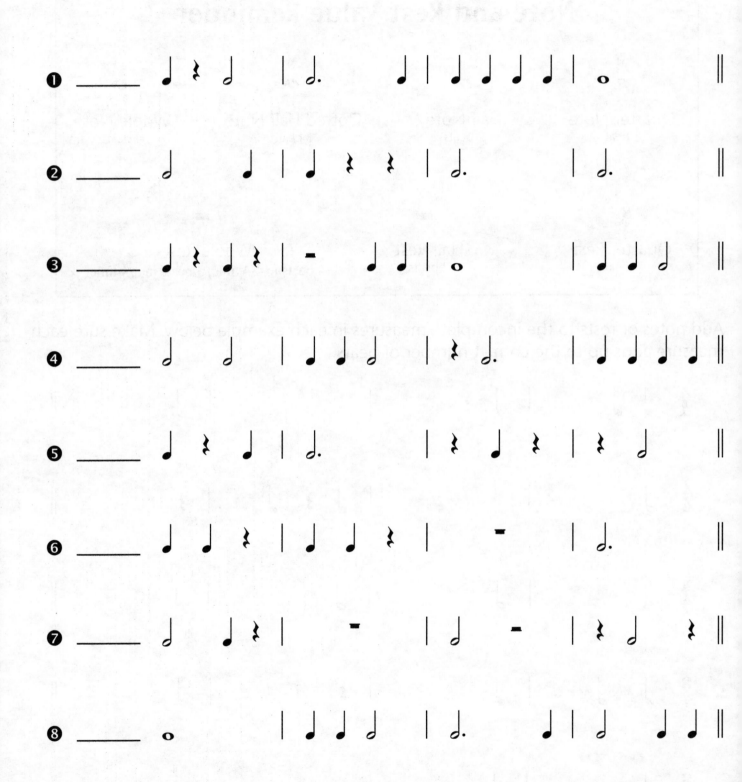

Read Between the Lines

The bar lines are missing in each example below. Add the bar lines to create measures that contain the correct number of beats, then write the counts under each measure.

For example,
you will be given:

Then you will write:

❶    

❷    

❸      

❹    

❺

❻    

30/2074H-29

Sign Posts

Study the note chart, then name each note on the sign posts below.

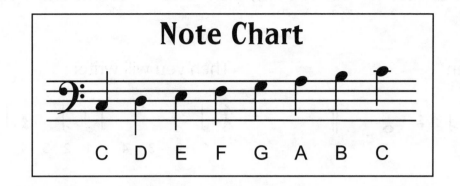

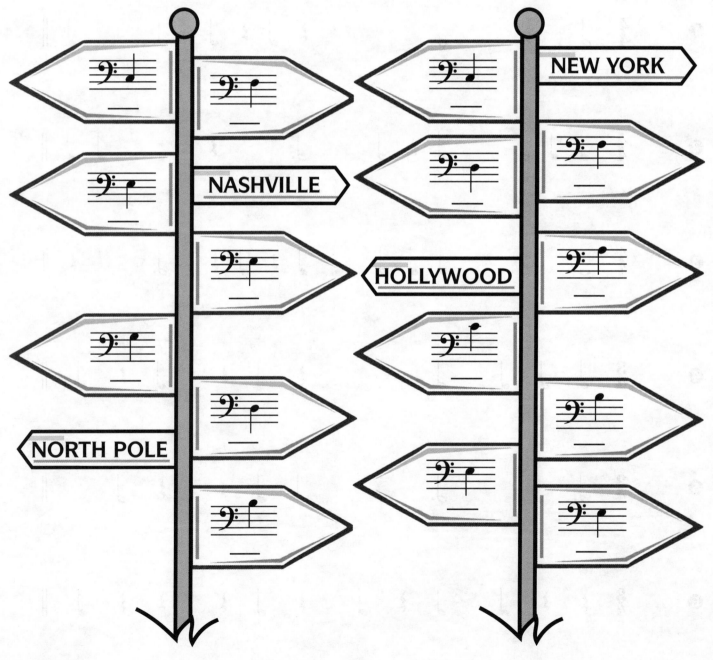

What's the Word?

Study the note chart below, then fill in the missing letters to solve each mystery word.

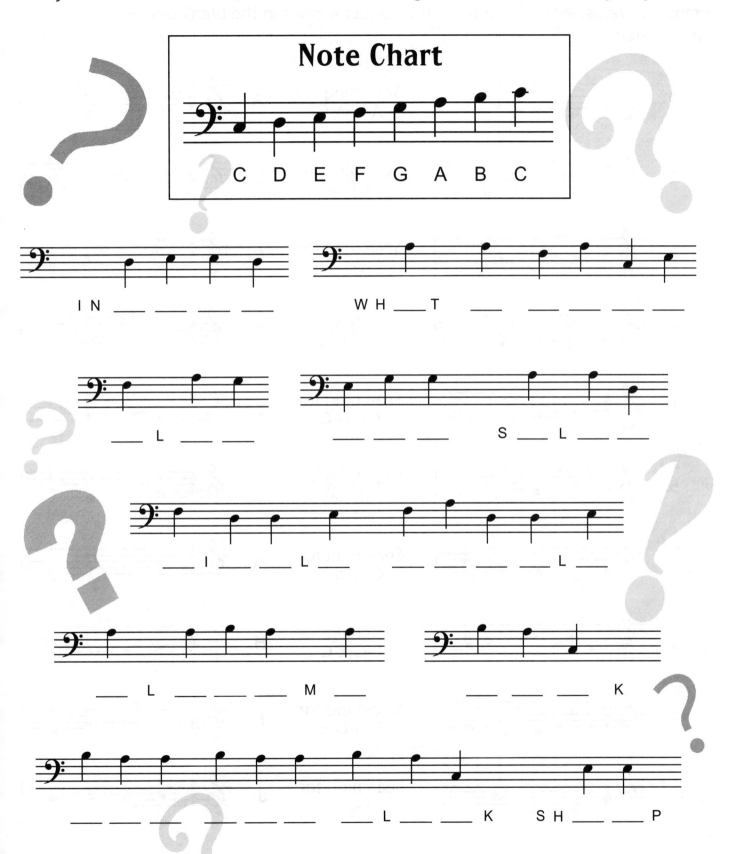

31

Missing Melodies

These melodies are in search of their missing notes. Follow the clues to complete these melodic phrases. Write the letter of the correct answer in the blank beside each number.

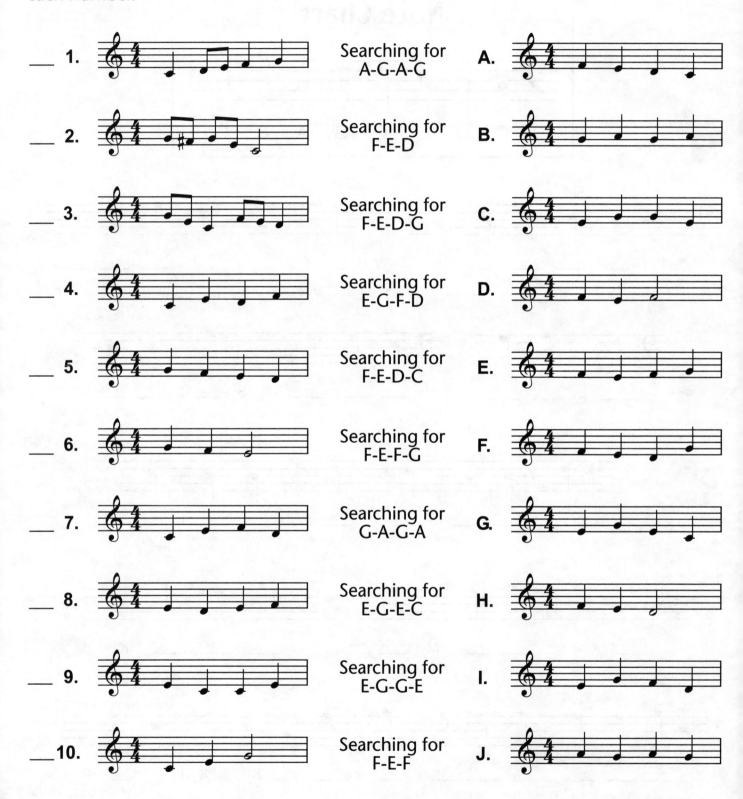

Rhythm Write-Up $\frac{4}{4}$

Your teacher will play a musical example for you that only uses quarter notes and half notes. As your teacher plays, bounce the tip of your pencil on each numbered beat. If you hear a note played on that beat, put a slash through that number. Then convert your slashes to notes. For example, your answer may look something like this:

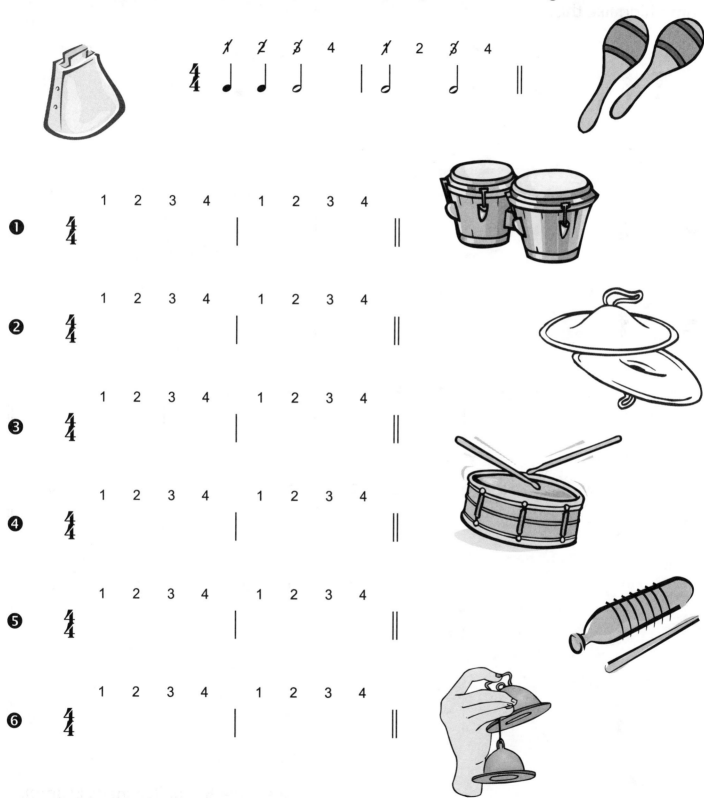

Rhythm Write-Up ¾

Your teacher will play several musical examples for you that only use quarter notes, half notes and dotted half notes. As your teacher plays, bounce the tip of your pencil on each numbered beat. If you hear a note played on that beat, put a slash through that number. Then convert your slashes to notes. For example, your answer may look something like this:

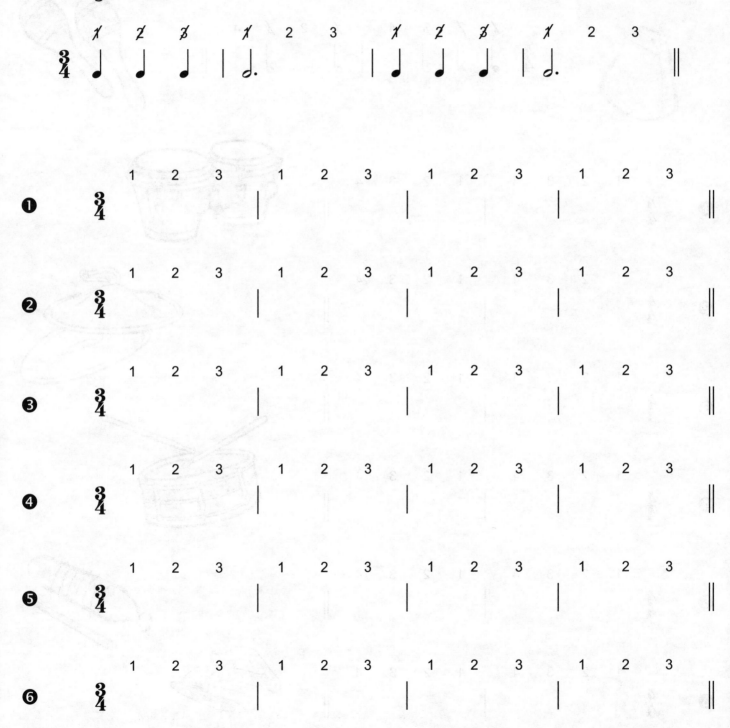

See page 86 for Teacher's Examples.

Take a Note

Your teacher will play a melody for you using only C and D half notes. Listen for notes moving up or down or repeating. As your teacher slowly plays the example, write down each note that you hear. The beginning note is given for you.

1.

2.

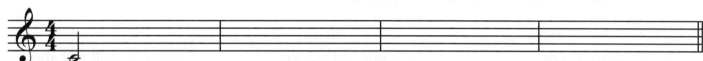

3.

Your teacher will play melodies for you using only C, D, and E half notes. Listen for notes moving up or down or repeating. As your teacher slowly plays the example, write down each note that you hear. These melodies will use only stepping motion or repeated notes (no skips). The beginning note is given for you.

4.

5.

6.

See pages 86 and 87 for Teacher's Examples.

30/2074H-35

Do-Re-Mi Dictation

Sing the following C Major scale with your teacher, using solfege (or syllables) for each note.

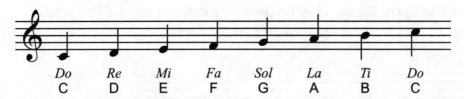

Your teacher will play little melodic phrases for you. Sing each one back with syllables. Then, using the chart above, turn each syllable that you sing into its corresponding note. Then notate your answer on the staff lines below.

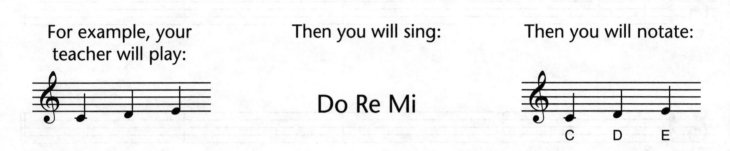

No time signatures are given for these examples. Just notate all notes as quarter notes. The beginning notes are given for you.

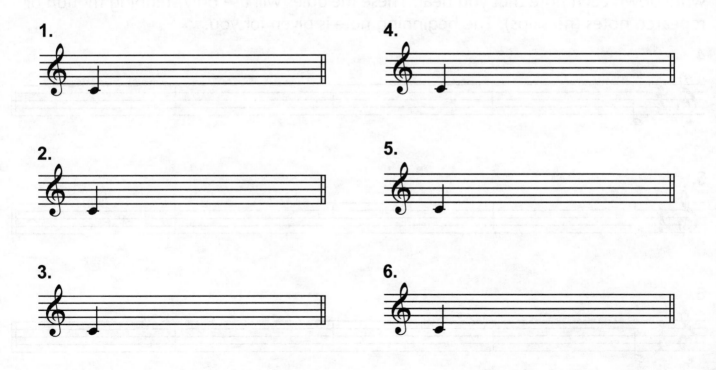

See page 87 for Teacher's Examples.

Follow the Bouncing Pencil

Your teacher will play musical examples for you that use quarter notes, half notes, dotted half notes and whole notes. As your teacher plays, bounce the tip of your pencil on each numbered beat. If you hear a note played on that beat, put a slash through that number. Then convert your slashes to notes. For example, your answer may look something like this:

See pages 87 and 88 for Teacher's Examples.

30/2074H-37

Two-Step Dictation

As your teacher plays the following musical examples for you, determine your answers with this two-step process. First, bounce the tip of your pencil on each numbered beat and put a slash through each beat played to determine the rhythms. Next, concentrate on the note names. Listen for steps, skips, or repeated notes. Also listen for notes moving up or notes moving down. Then match the rhythms you have heard. You may wish to use solfege to help you determine each pitch. For example your answer may look like this:

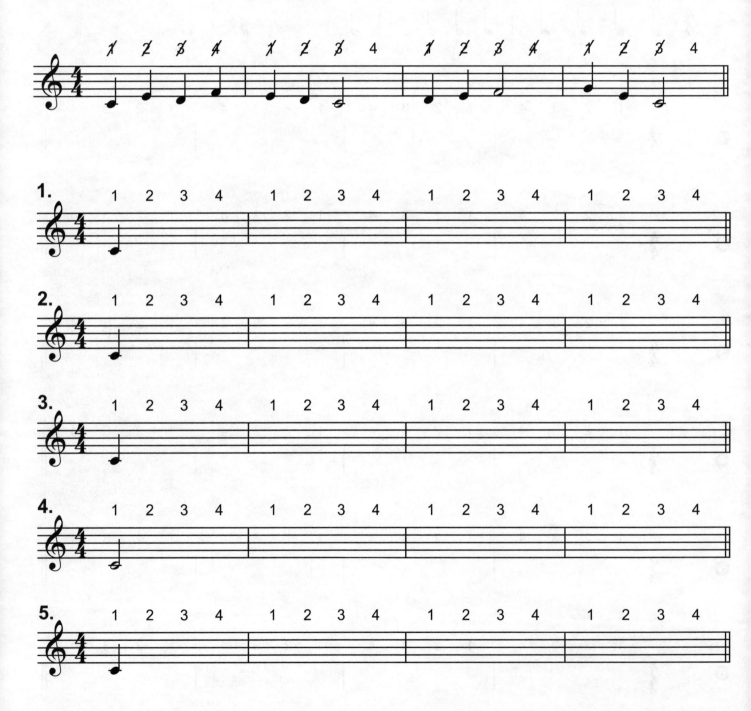

38   See page 88 for Teacher's Examples.

Add-a-Note Note Naming

Treble Clef

Begin by naming just two notes (C and D) in the first exercise below. Then add E in the next exercise, F in the next, G in the next, and A in the final exercise.

C   D

C   D   E

C   D   E   F

G

A

30/2074H-39

More Add-a-Note Note Naming   Treble Clef

Begin by naming just two notes (B and C) in the first exercise below. Then add D in the next exercise, E in the next, F in the next, and G in the final exercise.

B   C

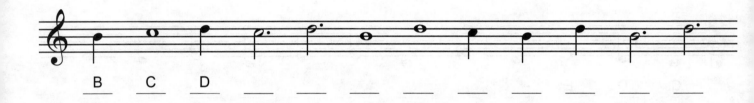

B   C   D

B   C   D   E

F

G

Summer Camp

Study the note chart below, then fill in the mystery words to complete this summer camp letter.

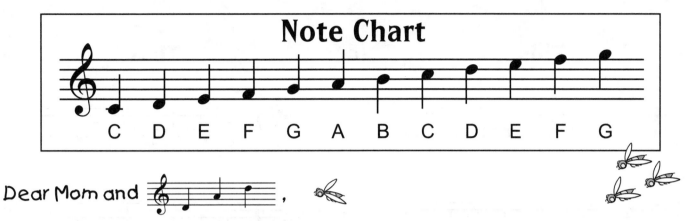

Note Chart

C D E F G A B C D E F G

Dear Mom and [＿ ＿ ＿],

I've only been at camp for three days, but I've already filled up my laundry [＿ ＿ ＿ ＿]. That's because the rain plus all the hiking [＿ ＿ ＿] up to lots of mud. Can you send me clean clothes and an umbrella? Thanks.

My [＿ ＿ ＿] is mostly comfortable, except for the corn flakes that my cabin mates put in it. We are studying bugs, because there are lots of them.

I drew a picture of a [＿ ＿ ＿] yesterday. They [＿ ＿ ＿ ＿] us pretty well. If you don't like the meal, you can just eat cookies. We had an [＿ ＿ ＿] toss the other day. (How do you get eggs out of your hair?)

We made a [＿ ＿ ＿ ＿] and shell necklace. Did you know beads work well with sling shots? Gotta go. We're doing [＿ ＿ ＿ ＿] painting today. I think the paint eventually comes off. Bye for now! Miss you!

P.S. I promise to [＿ ＿ ＿] good.

30/2074H-41

This or That

Compare each pair of musical examples. Your teacher will play only one of them.
Circle the example your teacher plays.

This *or* **That**

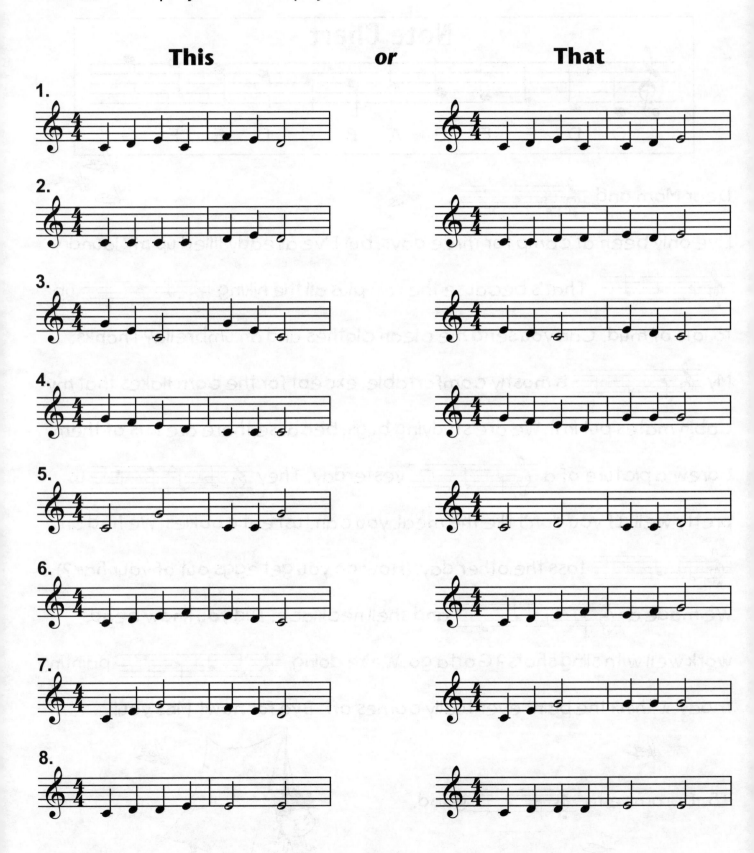

One or the Other

Compare each pair of rhythmic examples. Your teacher will play only one of them.
Circle the example your teacher plays.

One ***or*** **the Other**

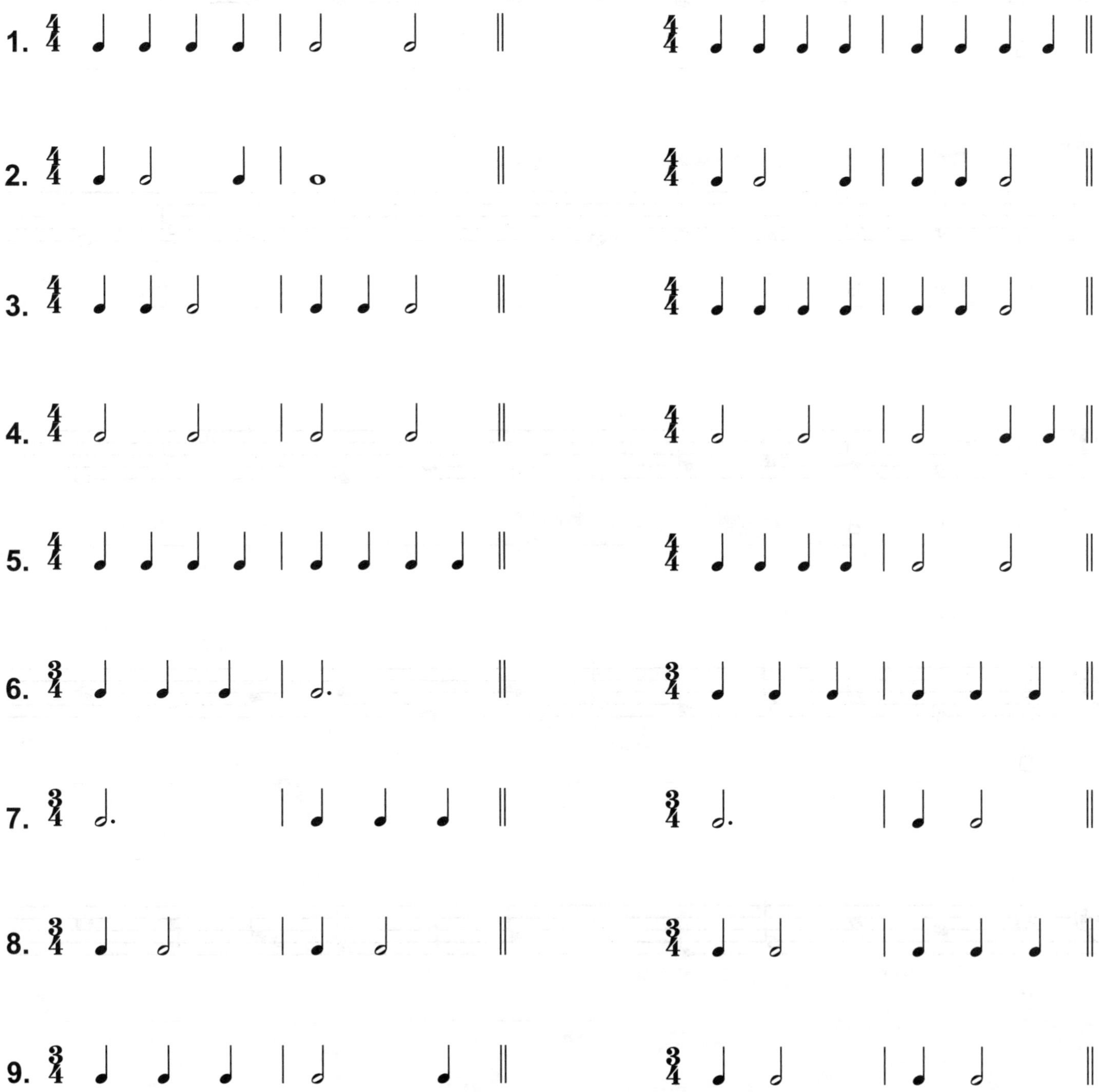

Note to Teacher: Play the examples using single note combinations of your choice.

Add-A-Note Note Naming

Bass Clef

Begin by naming just two notes (G and A) in the first exercise below. Then add B in the next exercise, C in the next, D in the next, and E in the final exercise.

G   A   __   __   __   __   __   __   __   __   __   __

G   A   B   __   __   __   __   __   __   __   __   __

G   A   B   C   __   __   __   __   __   __   __   __

D   __   __   __   __   __   __   __   __   __   __   __

E   __   __   __   __   __   __   __   __   __   __   __

More Add-A-Note Note Naming

Bass Clef

Begin by naming just two notes (F and G) in the first exercise below. Then add A in the next exercise, B in the next, and C in the next. On the final staff, put all your bass clef note-naming skills to the test.

F   G

F   G   A

F   G   A   B

C

30/2074H-45

Happy Birthday to Me

Study the note chart below, then fill in the mystery words to complete this letter to "Grandma" about birthday wishes.

Note Chart

G A B C D E F G A B C

Dear Grandma,

Mom said you called to ask me what I want for my birthday. Mom said a

book is always a good present, but if it's okay with you I'd like a dog of any

_____ ; but a puppy would be great. I'd name him _____ , or

if it's a girl dog, _____ I don't think Mom would mind if the puppy

slept with me in my _____ and in the morning he could lick my

_____ and wake me up. I'd play with him, _____

him doggy biscuits and we'd sit on the _____ of the front porch

steps and watch the world go by. I bet I could even teach him to roll over

or sit up and _____ . I can see it now. He'd become famous, star in

a T.V. show and would _____ the most sought after dog in the world.

I'd get my picture taken with him and we'd be on an _____ together for

dog food. We'd make enough money to pay for my college. Well, gotta go. I

have to clean my room before _____ gets home! Love ya! Bye!

Right or Wrong?

A new music student has named each note below, but still needs a little help learning their notes. Cross out any incorrect answers and write in the correct name of those notes.

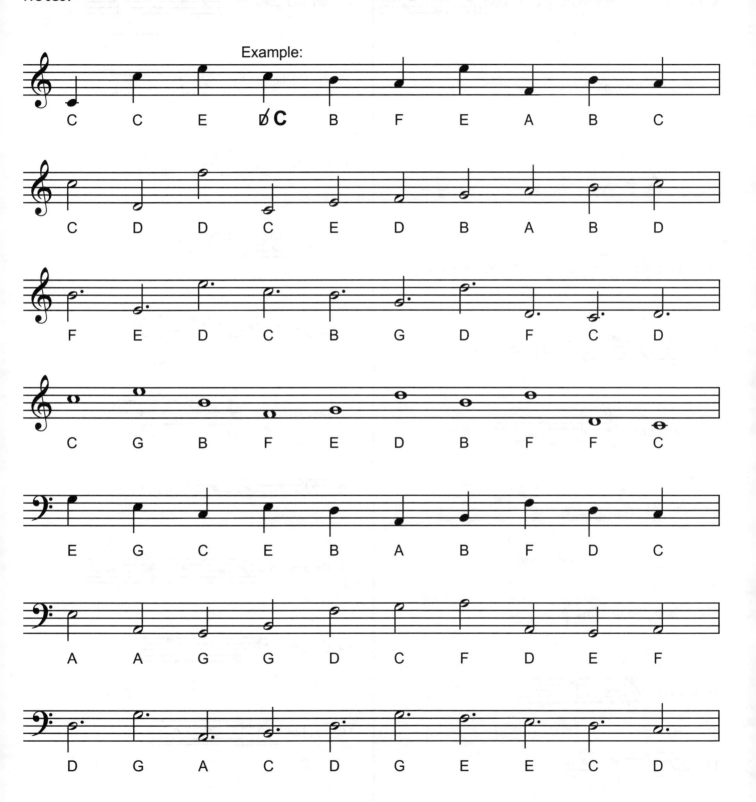

47

Keynote Crossword Clues

Across

3. I taught my puppy to sit up and

4. Opie's Aunt

6. Can I carry your

8. A _____ for my necklace

10. _____ the birds

12. Subtract or

13. The tides _____ and flowed

15. To be or not to

16. Canopy

17. _____ whiz

Down

1. Can you guess my

2. The chicken or the

3. It's in the

5. Honest

7. The gift of

9. I take after my

10. _____ Fi Fo Fum

11. Do a good

14. Laundry

15. Bumble

Keynote Crossword

Use the note clues to solve this crossword puzzle. Every answer uses only notes from the musical alphabet: A B C D E F G.

Fast Facts: Johann Sebastian Bach

* Bach was a German composer who lived from 1685-1750.
* Along with George Frideric Handel, he is one of the most noted composers of the Baroque Period.
* As a child he learned the violin from his father.
* His brother taught him how to play the clavichord.
* He copied by hand other composers' works to study their compositional style.
* He dazzled the audiences of his time with his great improvisational skills.
* Even Frederick the Great was impressed with his performances.
* For many years he was musical director at St. Thomas School in Leipzig.
* Among his most famous works are the six *Brandenburg Concertos*.
* He is also especially known for his keyboard works, including his *Inventions* and *The Well-Tempered Clavier* (a set of preludes and fugues).
* He composed a large body of sacred music, including 100 church cantatas, the two great Passions (*St. Matthew* and *St. John*) and his *Mass in B minor*.
* He was married twice and had 20 children.
* Many of his children went on to be musicians and composers who actually enjoyed greater fame than their father did in his lifetime.
* For nearly a hundred years his works were largely unknown until the composer Felix Mendelssohn Bartholdy introduced European audiences to Bach's works.

Study and read the Bach facts above, then cover them up and test your memory. See how many of the questions you can answer. The first letter of each answer is given for you.

❶ Bach was a G_____ composer who lived from 1685-1750.

❷ Along with George Frideric H_____, Bach is one of the most prominent composers of the B_____ Period.

❸ His father taught him the v_____.

❹ His brother taught him the c_____.

❺ He impressed audiences with his i_____ skills.

❻ Even Frederick the G_____ was impressed with Bach's playing.

❼ His set of preludes and fugues is known as *The W_____-T_____
C_____*.

❽ *St. Matthew* and *St. John* are the titles of his two great P_____.

❾ Felix Mendelssohn Bartholdy introduced E_____ audiences to Bach's works nearly a hundred years after Bach had composed them.

Johann Sebastian Bach

Abbreviated Themes

Boureé in E Minor

Sheep May Safely Graze

from Cantata No. 205

Minuet in G Major

Fast Facts: Ludwig van Beethoven

* Born in Bonn, Germany
* Lived from 1770-1827
* Bridged the gap from the Classical Period to the Romantic Period
* Mozart said of Beethoven, "He will give the world something worth listening to."
* Count Waldstein was his life-long patron.
* Beethoven composed many of his works while living in Vienna.
* At the age of 30, he began to grow deaf.
* Composed some of this greatest works after he had completely lost his hearing.
* His sketch-books of his compositional ideas still exist today.
* Among his many famous works are *Ode to Joy, Für Elise*, the *Moonlight Sonata* and his opera, *Fidelio.*
* He composed 9 symphonies, including the *Pastorale* and *Eroica*, numerous choral works and 30 sonatas for the piano.

Study and read the Beethoven facts above, then cover them up and test your memory. See how many of the questions below you can answer. The first letter of each answer is given for you.

❶ Beethoven was born in B _____, G_____.

❷ Beethoven bridged the gap from the C_____ period to the R_____ period.

❸ M_____ said of Beethoven, "He will give the world something worth listening to."

❹ Beethoven's life-long patron was Count W_____.

❺ Beethoven did much of his composing in the city of V_____.

❻ Later in his life, Beethoven composed many magnificent works, even though he was d_____.

❼ His s_____-_____ of his compositional ideas still exist today.

❽ One of his most famous pieces is called *Ode to J_____.*

❾ One of his most famous sonatas is known as the *M_____ Sonata.*

❿ His opera is called *F_____.*

Ludwig van Beethoven

Abbreviated Themes

Turkish March
from *The Ruins of Athens*

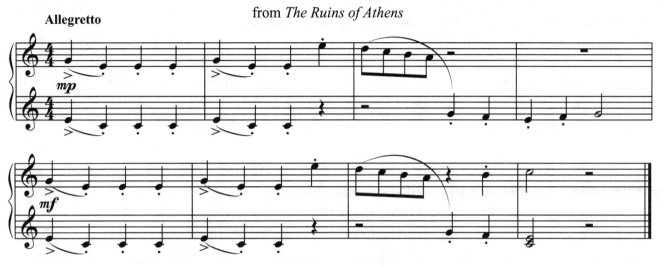

The Pastoral Symphony
Symphony No. 6, First Movement Theme

Für Elise

30/2074H-53

Fast Facts: Johannes Brahms

* Born in Hamburg on May 7, 1833 and died in Vienna on April 3, 1897
* Son and pupil of a double-bass player
* Made his debut as a performer at the age of 14 playing his own variations on a folk song
* As a young man, he performed with many other musicians in recitals, including Joachim, a prominent violinist, who introduced him to the famous composers, Franz Liszt and Robert Schumann.
* Robert Schumann proclaimed Brahms to be "the new messiah of music."
* Capturing the lush and rich melodic style of the Romantic Period, Brahms' music also reflected his interest in music from earlier times.
* He collected a large library of music and theoretical writing of the 1700's and earlier.
* He also particularly admired and studied the scores of Richard Wagner (1813-1883).
* Apart from his extensive composing career and performing throughout Europe as a pianist, he also conducted and composed music for many choirs, including a women's chorus in Hamburg which he founded.
* His wealth of compositions include his *German Requiem*, 4 symphonies, *The Academic Festival Overture*, numerous songs for voice and piano, chamber works, and solos for the piano.

Study and read the Brahms facts above, then cover them up and test your memory. See how many of the questions you can answer. The first letter of each answer is given for you.

❶ Brahms was born in H_____ in 1833 and died in V_____ in 1897.

❷ He was the son and pupil of a d_____ player.

❸ The violinist, Joachim, introduced him to two prominent composers of the day: Franz L_____ and Robert S_____.

❹ Schumann heralded Brahms to be "the new m_____ of music."

❺ Brahms' lush harmonies and rich melodies reflect the compositional style of the R_____ Period.

❻ Brahms studied music from much earlier times and also particularly admired the music of Richard W_____.

❼ He founded a w_____ chorus in Hamburg.

❽ His G_____ *Requiem* and his A_____ F_____ *Overture* are among his many famous works.

Johannes Brahms

Abbreviated Themes

Piano Concerto in B♭ Major
Second Movement Theme

Symphony No. 1
Chorale from the Fourth Movement

Academic Festival Overture
Gaudeamus Igitur

Fast Facts: George Frideric Handel

* German-born composer, lived from 1685-1759
* In 1703, he abandoned the study of law to become a violinist at the opera house in Hamburg
* Visits to Italy inspired him to compose a number of operas and oratorios.
* Throughout his composing career, he worked primarily in England.
* He became a British subject in 1726.
* One of his most famous works, *Water Music*, was written in 1717 for George I.
* His masterpiece, the *Messiah* (an oratorio), has the famous *Hallelujah Chorus* in it.
* The *Messiah* debuted in Dublin in 1742.
* Handel composed more than 25 oratorios throughout his career.
* His famous set of variations that he composed for the harpsichord is nicknamed *The Harmonious Blacksmith*.
* Along with Johann Sebastian Bach, he is considered to be a master of the Baroque Period.
* The day before he died, he conducted a Holy Week performance of *Messiah*. Handel is buried in Westminster Abbey in London.

Study and read the Handel facts above, then cover them up and test your memory. See how many of the questions you can answer. The first letter of each answer is given for you.

❶ Handel was a G_____-born composer.

❷ In 1703, he abandoned the study of l_____.

❸ Visits to I_____ inspired him to write a number of operas and oratorios.

❹ Throughout his composing career, he worked primarily in E_____.

❺ He composed his famous *Water Music* for King G_____.

❻ His famous oratorio, the M_____ debuted in Dublin in 1742.

❽ Perhaps the best-known piece from the *Messiah* is the H_____ C_____.

❼ Along with Johann Sebastian B_____, Handel is considered to be a master of the B_____ P_____.

❽ Handel is buried in L_____ at W_____ A_____.

George Frideric Handel

Abbreviated Themes

See, the Conquering Hero Comes
from *Judas Maccabaeus*

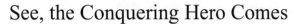

Hornpipe
from *Water Music*

Hallelujah Chorus
from *Messiah*

Fast Facts: Franz Joseph Haydn

* Haydn lived from 1732-1809.
* Along with Mozart, he was one of the most important composers of the Classical Period.
* At the age of 5, he went to live with his cousin who taught him Latin, singing, the violin and other instruments.
* At the age of 9, he went to Vienna for further musical instruction.
* By the age of 13, he had composed a mass.
* As a young teen, he rented a small attic room and a harpsichord to practice the works of the famous composers of his day.
* As an adult he flourished as a composer under the patronage of Prince Paul Anton Esterhazy.
* At one point, Beethoven was one of his pupils.
* Haydn composed 125 symphonies and overtures, including the *Farewell* and *Surprise Symphony*.
* Among his numerous works are 77 string quartets, 14 masses, 4 operas, several keyboard works and his famous oratorio, *The Creation*.

Study and read the Haydn facts above, then cover them up and test your memory. See how many of the questions below you can answer. The first letter of each answer is given for you.

❶ Along with Wolfgang Amadeus M_____, Haydn was one of the most important composers of the C_____ Period.

❷ At the age of 5, he went to live with his c_____ who taught him not only singing and instruments, but L_____ as well.

❸ At the age of 9 he went to live in V_____ for further musical instruction.

❹ By the age of 13 he had composed his first m_____.

❺ As a young teen, he practiced famous keyboard works on a h_____.

❻ Prince Paul Anton E_____ was Haydn's life-long patron.

❼ Two of his most famous symphonies are the *F_____ Symphony* and the *S_____ Symphony*.

❽ He composed 77 s_____ q_____.

❾ His famous oratorio is called *The C_____*.

Franz Joseph Haydn

Abbreviated Themes

The Surprise Symphony, Symphony No. 94
Andante, Second Movement Theme

Serenade
from *String Quartet,* Op. 3, No. 5

Gypsy Rondo

30/2074H-59

Fast Facts: Wolfgang Amadeus Mozart

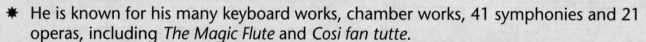

* Born in Salzburg, Austria
* Lived from 1756-1791
* One of the most important composers of the Classical Period
* A true child prodigy; by the age of 9, he had written his first symphony.
* Also as a child, he performed for the royalty of Europe with his sister, Nannerl.
* They made their joint debut together in Munich, Germany when Mozart was barely 6 years old.
* Despite his genius, as an adult, he struggled to maintain his career.
* He is known for his many keyboard works, chamber works, 41 symphonies and 21 operas, including *The Magic Flute* and *Cosi fan tutte*.
* A famous chamber work of his is *Eine kleine Nachtmusik* (A Little Night Music).
* He married Constance Weber in 1782. Together they had 6 children.

Study and read the Mozart facts above, then cover them up and test your memory. See how many of the questions below you can answer. The first letter of each answer is given for you.

❶ Mozart was born in S_____, A_____.

❷ Mozart is one of the most important composers of the C_____ Period.

❸ He was a true child p_____.

❹ By the age of 9, he had written his first s_____.

❺ He performed throughout Europe with his sister, N_____.

❻ As an adult, he struggled to maintain his c_____.

❼ He composed 41 s_____ and 21 o_____.

❽ One of his most famous operas is called *The M_____ F_____*.

❾ His chamber work *Eine kleine Nachtmusik* is translated into English as
A L_____ N_____ M_____.

❿ In 1782, he married Constance W_____.

Wolfgang Amadeus Mozart
Abbreviated Themes

Rondo
from *Eine kleine Nachtmusik*

Tamino's Aria
from *The Magic Flute*

Symphony No. 40
First Movement Theme

61

Fast Facts: Franz Schubert

* Austrian-born, lived from 1797-1828
* Son of a schoolmaster who taught him the violin
* As a young boy, he sang first soprano in the church choir.
* By the age of 16, he had composed his first symphony.
* Captured the style of the Romantic Period with his rich and memorable melodies
* Schubert wrote over 600 German songs or *Lieder* in his short lifetime.
* His famous song collections or cycles are called Die schöne Mullerin (The Beautiful Maid) 1823 and Die Winterreisse (The Winter Journey) 1827.
* For lyrics of his songs, he used the famous poems of his day, including those by Goethe and Schiller.
* His compositions influenced later Romantic composers of song such as the famous Robert Schumann.
* An extraordinarily prolific composer, Schubert composed numerous works for piano, string quartets and quintets, among which is his famous *Trout Quintet*.
* Of his 9 symphonies, his best-known is actually only 2 movements, appropriately named the *Unfinished Symphony*.

Study and read the Schubert facts above, then cover them up and test your memory. See how many of the questions you can answer. The first letter of each answer is given for you.

❶ Franz Schubert was born in A_____.

❷ His father, a schoolmaster, taught him to play the v_____.

❸ As a young boy, he sang first s_____ in a church choir.

❹ By the age of 16, he had composed his first s_____.

❺ Interestingly enough, his most famous symphony is the *U_____ Symphony* which only has 2 movements.

❻ Schubert is particularly famous for his German songs or L_____.

❼ For lyrics for these songs he used famous p_____ of his day, like those by G_____ and Schiller.

❽ His song style influenced many famous composers of the Romantic period, including Robert S_____.

❾ One of his best-known and most playful of his chamber works is called *The T_____ Quintet.*

Franz Schubert
Abbreviated Themes

March Militaire

The Unfinished Symphony, Symphony No. 8
Moderato Movement

The Trout Quintet
Fourth Movement Theme

30/2074H-63

Fast Facts: Igor Stravinsky

* Russian-born composer, lived from 1882-1971
* Began piano lessons at the age of 9
* Studied composition and orchestration with the famous composer, Nikolai Rimsky-Korsakov from 1903-1908
* Actually never attended music school or a conservatory
* Along with Arnold Schoenberg, regarded as one of the most influential composers of the twentieth century
* Gained world fame for his three major ballets, all based on Russian folklore: *The Firebird* (1910) *Petrouchka* (1911, then revised in 1947), and *The Rite of Spring* (Le Sacre du Printemps, 1913)
* Because of its huge orchestrations, jagged and insistent rhythms, and innovative harmonies, *The Rite of Spring* caused a riot at its first performance.
* From 1919-1951, Stravinsky composed in the Neoclassical style, modeling his pieces on works from the past, using themes from Italian Baroque music and composing an opera (*The Rake's Progress*) stylistically similar to Mozart.
* Eventually adapted the 12-tone basis of composing in his own unique way, especially evident in his work, *In Memoriam Dylan Thomas* (1954)
* Stravinsky left Russia in 1914, first living in Switzerland and ultimately becoming a citizen of both France (1934) and the United States (1945).

Study and read the Stravinsky facts above, then cover them up and test your memory. See how many of the questions you can answer. The first letter of each answer is given for you.

❶ Stravinsky was born in R_____ in 1882.

❷ He became a citizen of F_____ and the U _____ S_____.

❸ Stravinsky is considered one of the most important composers of the T_____ Century.

❹ He studied composition and orchestration with the famous composer, Nikolai R_____-K_____.

❺ He gained world fame with his three major b_____.

❻ His ballet, *The R_____ of S_____* actually caused a riot with its first performance.

❼ His ballets are based upon Russian f_____.

❽ From 1919-1951, Stravinsky composed music in the N_____ style and then adapted his own version of 12-t_____ composing.

Igor Stravinsky

Abbreviated Themes

Russian Dance
from *Petrushka*

Finale
from *The Firebird Suite*

30/2074H-65

Fast Facts: Peter Ilyich Tchaikovsky

* Russian-born, lived from 1840-1893
* First Russian composer to become well-known to Western audiences
* Did not take up music seriously until he was 22
* Before that, he studied law and worked at a post in the government civil service.
* As a young man, he entered the newly founded St. Petersburg Conservatory where he later became a professor of harmony.
* In 1889, he visited New York for the dedication of the new Carnegie Hall where he performed his own compositions.
* He was, in particular, a great admirer of Mozart.
* A composer of the Romantic and late Romantic period, Tchaikovsky is known for his sense of melody, personal expression and brilliant orchestrations.
* Among his many works are 11 Russian operas, 6 symphonies, including his famous *Pathetique* and 3 overtures, including the *1812 Overture* which often uses real canons in performance.
* His very popular ballets include *Swan Lake*, *The Sleeping Beauty*, and *The Nutcracker* which is often performed at Christmas time.
* His memorable piano concertos also remain a favorite of audiences today.

Study and read the Tchaikovsky facts above, then cover them up and test your memory. See how many of the questions you can answer. The first letter of each answer is given for you.

❶ Tchaikovsky was born in R_____.

❷ He composed music during the R_____ Period.

❸ Before he seriously pursued music, he studied l_____ .

❹ As a young man, he entered the newly founded St. P_____ Conservatory where he later became a professor of h_____.

❺ In 1889, he visited N_____ Y_____ for the dedication of the new C_____ Hall.

❻ Among his 6 symphonies is the famous P_____ *Symphony*.

❼ His *1812 O_____* often uses real canons in performance.

❽ His famous ballets include *S_____ Lake* and *S_____ Beauty*.

❾ His ballet, *The N_____* is often performed at Christmas time.

Peter Ilyich Tchaikovsky
Abbreviated Themes

Swan Lake
Theme

Sleeping Beauty
Waltz

Dance of the Sugarplum Fairy
from *The Nutcracker*

30/2074H-67

Fast Facts: Richard Wagner

* A German composer who lived from 1813-1883
* Changed the course of music and theatrical history
* Believed that theatre should be the center of a community's culture and not just a place of entertainment
* Eventually built his own theatre and founded Europe's oldest summer music festival
* Wagner wrote his own opera librettos (the text).
* He based his operas upon historical events, medieval myths and legends.
* His operas were unique. Instead of traditional works which featured a series of separate songs, Wagner's operas were a free-flowing chain of musical ideas or motives and various key signatures creating very large musical dramas.
* In addition to his composing and libretto writing, Wagner wrote essays which outlined and defended the principles of his musical dramas.
* His career, personal life and finances were often stormy and unsettled. He even participated in a social revolution in Germany in 1849 which led to a warrant for his arrest. He fled to Switzerland and was only allowed to return to Germany 12 years later.
* In 1864, after many years of financial hardship, King Ludwig II of Bavaria came to his rescue and Wagner became one of the king's advisors.
* Among his many works are the operas *Lohengrin, Rienzi* (composed after hearing a performance of Beethoven's Ninth Symphony) *The Flying Dutchman, Tannhauser, Tristan and Isolde,* and *The Ring of the Nibelung*, a cycle of 4 operas including *Die Walküre*.

Study and read the Wagner facts above, then cover them up and test your memory. See how many of the questions you can answer. The first letter of each answer is given for you.

❶ Wagner was born in G_____ , although in 1849 he fled to S_____ after a warrant was sworn out for his arrest.

❷ He changed the course of music and t_____ history.

❸ Wagner believed that theatre should be the center of a community's c_____.

❹ He founded Europe's oldest s_____ m_____ f_____.

❺ Wagner wrote his own l_____ or text for his operas.

❻ Wagner also wrote e_____ which defended the principles of his music dramas.

❼ King L_____ II of B_____ helped save Wagner from financial ruin.

❽ He composed the opera, *Rienzi*, after hearing a performance of B_____ Ninth Symphony.

❾ The *Ring of the Nibelung* is a c_____ of 4 operas that he composed.

Richard Wagner

Abbreviated Themes

Bridal March

from *Lohengrin*

Overture

from *Die Walküre*

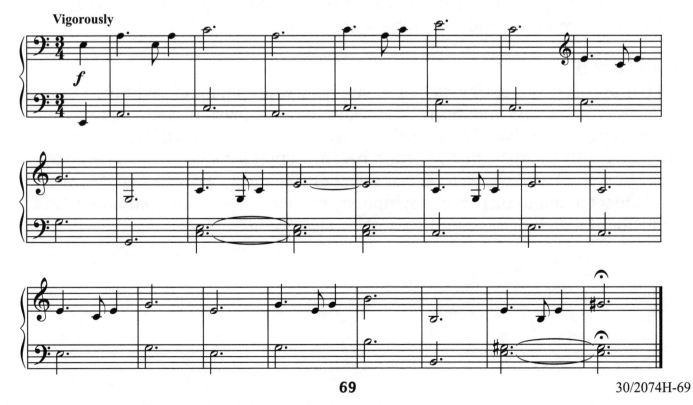

30/2074H-69

Style Dictionary

Your teacher will discuss and play for you examples of the following musical styles:

The Minuet

For nearly a century, the minuet was the most popular couple's dance of European Royal Courts and high society from the late 1600's to the late 1700's. Couples dance to the stately gentile music in 3/4 time, moving along in a route in the form of an S or a Z. The minuet was first developed in the court of King Louis XIV of France. Minuets also appear in many operas and ballets and later the term often described one of the movements of a longer piece such as a symphony or a sonata.

The Waltz

The waltz is a dance in 3/4 time with a lilting feel. Historically, it was very popular in the 1800's and actually was once considered to be scandalous for couples to dance so closely together as they glided and turned across the dance floor. Many composers of the 1800's and 1900's wrote waltzes just for listening rather than dancing. Famous waltz composers include Johann Strauss Jr., Frederic Chopin and you'll also find waltzes in famous ballets such as Tchaikovsky's *Swan Lake*.

The Polka

The polka is a brisk and lively dance in 2/4 time. The basic step is a hop followed by three short steps. The polka was originally a Czech peasant dance, developed in Eastern Bohemia, using folk song tunes. The dance was first introduced to the ballrooms of Prague in 1835. In 1840, the dance was introduced to Paris audiences and became wildly popular. Even today the polka remains popular in such genres as Country Western polkas and within the American/European cultures.

The March

March music is a form of classical music originally written for and performed by military bands. History finds armies marching to music (even played by just a simple drum, flute or bagpipe) to maintain their spirits and morale. The marches' strong beat and energetic rhythms soon became a popular style for solo keyboard and instrumental works as well. Earlier marches, like those of Beethoven, Mozart and Handel tended to be part of a symphony or suite. The greatest composer and conductor of march music is probably John Philip Sousa.

Ragtime

Ragtime pieces are highly rhythmic and playful pieces, especially popular in the United States from around 1895-1915. Their name comes from "ragged time," often simply called rags. The melodies are syncopated with accents on the off-beats accompanied by the "tick-tock" evenness of the accompaniment. Rags were either played by piano or by small bands and became an early influence of jazz pieces. The best-known composer of rags is Scott Joplin.

The Blues

A rich heritage and history lies behind the blues. It first began in African-American music in the rural south in the late 19th century characterized by a 12-bar (measures) construction and melancholy lyrics. In the 1920's and 1930's the rural or delta blues were performed often on guitar or harmonica. In the 1940's and 1950's it took on urban sounds, using electric instruments, captured especially by musicians in Chicago. In the 1960's it grew in even greater popularity with music performed by B.B. King, inspiring British musician, Eric Clapton.

Jazz Ballads

In the 1930's and 1940's jazz musicians softened the tones of their instruments, played syncopated rhythms in a more laid-back style and in general played with a more even beat. Slow romantic solos, like those played by saxophonist Stan Getz influenced younger jazz musicians like Miles Davis and Gil Evans. These soft instrumental sounds along with a lazy tempo and unusual orchestrations are sometimes referred to as "cool jazz."

Boogie-Woogie

The boogie-woogie is a type of jazz piece played on the piano where the left hand bops along with a repeated pattern, much like the notes an upright-bass player would play in a jazz combo. It was particularly popular in the United States from around the 1900's – 1950's. The boogie-woogie style also influenced early rock and roll.

New Age

New Age music was especially popular in the 1980's. A type of instrumental music, it is very fluid, reflective, and often dream-like in the mood that it sets. It is far less insistent than rock and is often performed acoustically (un-amplified) or on an electric instrument featuring mellow and soft tones. In 1975, guitarist William Ackerman (founder of the Windham Hill record label) coined the term "new-age music" which refers to a spiritual mood of the generation of people that embraced these smooth and soothing sounds. New age music often incorporates sounds of nature.

30/2074H-71

I Think I Hear a Waltz

Your teacher will play nine musical examples for you. Choose from the following lists of musical styles and select the answer that best matches each example you hear.

A. Minuet   **B.** Waltz   **C.** Polka   **D.** March   **E.** Ragtime

F. Blues   **G.** Jazz Ballads   **H.** Boogie-Woogie   **I.** New Age

Example 1 _____

Example 2 _____

Example 3 _____

Example 4 _____

Example 5 _____

Example 6 _____

Example 7 _____

Example 8 _____

Example 9 _____

Note to Teacher: Play the examples in any order you wish from those presented on pages 75-83.

Style Match-Up

Match the following descriptions to their corresponding style. You may use each style more than once if necessary.

> **A.** Minuet **B.** Waltz **C.** Polka **D.** March **E.** Ragtime
>
> **F.** Blues **G.** Jazz Ballads **H.** Boogie-Woogie **I.** New Age

1. _____ Began with African-American music in the rural south.

2. _____ A type of jazz piece played on the piano where the left hand plays a repeated pattern.

3. _____ Very fluid, reflective and dream-like.

4. _____ A dance in 3/4 time with a lilting feel.

5. _____ A popular couple's dance of the European Royal Courts.

6. _____ Originally written for and performed by military bands.

7. _____ First developed in the court of King Louis XIV of France.

8. _____ The greatest composer of this style is John Philip Sousa.

9. _____ Originally a Czech peasant piece.

10. _____ In the 1920's, this style was often performed on the guitar or harmonica.

11. _____ Stan Getz and Miles Davis are players associated with this style.

12. _____ Often incorporates sounds of nature.

13. _____ The melodies are syncopated with accents on the off-beats.

14. _____ The best-known composer of this style is Scott Joplin.

15. _____ In the 1960's, performer B.B. King drew special attention to this style.

16. _____ This style was first introduced to the ballrooms of Prague in 1835.

17. _____ Johann Strauss was a popular composer of this style.

18. _____ A dance that moves along in the form of an S or Z.

Style Choice

Complete each fact by choosing from the following styles:

1. In the 1700's, couples danced to the stately gentile music of the a) minuet
    b) march c) polka.

2. Folk tunes from Eastern Bohemia became the musical foundation of the a) waltz
    b) march c) polka.

3. Miles Davis and Gil Evans are often associated with their performances of
    a) new age music b) ragtime c) jazz ballads.

4. The repeated left-hand patterns drive the style and tempo of a) jazz ballads
    b) new age music c) boogie-woogie.

5. B.B. King inspired Eric Clapton to play and perform the a) minuet   b) new age
    music c) blues.

6. In the 1930's, musicians performed in the laid-back style of a) jazz ballads
    b) ragtime c) marches.

7. Guitarist William Ackerman of Windham Hill Records coined the phrase
    a) boogie-woogie b) new age music c) ragtime.

8. To lift their morale and spirits, history finds armies charging forward to the
    sounds of the a) polka b) march c) minuet.

9. Around 1835, the ballrooms of Prague were filled with the sounds of the
    a) polka b) march c) minuet.

10. Early in its popularity, it was considered very scandalous for couples to dance the
    a) polka b) minuet c) waltz.

11. Sounds of nature are often incorporated into a) jazz ballads b) new age music
    c) the blues.

12. Scott Joplin is the best-known composer of a) rags b) marches c) jazz ballads.

13. John Philip Sousa is especially known for composing a) polkas b) ragtime
    c) marches.

14. The basic dance step of a hop followed by three short steps is performed by
    couples as they dance the a) minuet b) polka c) waltz.

15. Couples glided across the dance floor to Johann Strauss' a) minuets b) polkas
    c) waltzes.

Minuet Examples

Minuet in F Major
Franz Joseph Haydn

Minuet in D Minor
Jean-Baptiste Lully

Minuet in G Minor
Johann Sebastian Bach

30/2074H-75

Waltz Examples

Blue Danube Waltz
Johann Strauss, Jr.

Waltz from Swan Lake
Peter Ilyich Tchaikovsky

Musetta's Waltz from La Bohème
Giacomo Puccini

Polka Examples

Polka-Dots
Janet Vogt

Polka Party
Janet Vogt

Peasant Dance Polka
Janet Vogt

March Examples

March Militaire
Franz Schubert

Funeral March of the Marionette
Charles Gounod

March
Jeremiah Clarke

Ragtime Examples

The Entertainer
Scott Joplin

Tick Tock Rag
Janet Vogt

Bumblebee Rag
Janet Vogt

30/2074H-79

The Blues Examples

Turquoise Blues
Barbara Lopez

Too Bad Blues!
Walter and Carol Noona

Jazz Ballad Examples

The Last Time I Saw You
Janet Vogt

Prelude in F
Walter and Carol Noona

Boogie-Woogie Examples

Tiger Beetle Boogie
Steve Nehrenburg

On Track Boogie
Walter and Carol Noona

New Age Examples

The Brook and Beyond
Janet Vogt

Spring Rain
Steve Nehrenburg

30/2074H-83

Either Or (page 7)

Up, Down and All Around (page 9)

The Same or Different? (page 10)

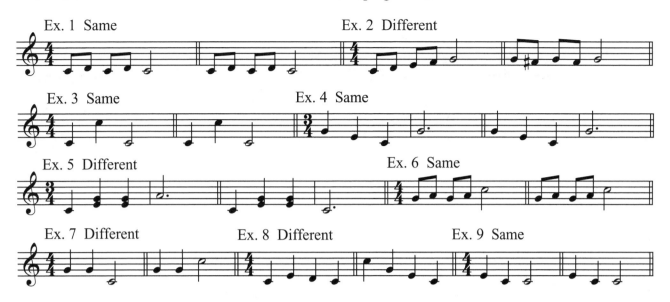

Next Note: Higher or Lower (page 11)

Next Note: Step or Skip (page 21)

Rhythm Write-Up 𝄴 (page 33)

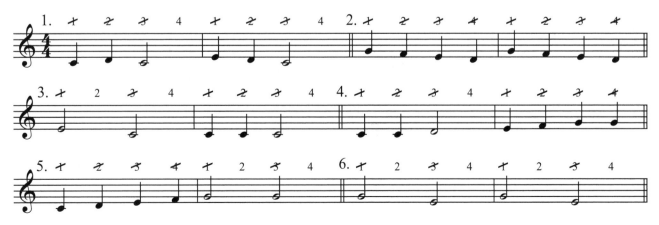

Rhythm Write-Up ¾ (page 34)

Take a Note (page 35)

(Continued on next page)

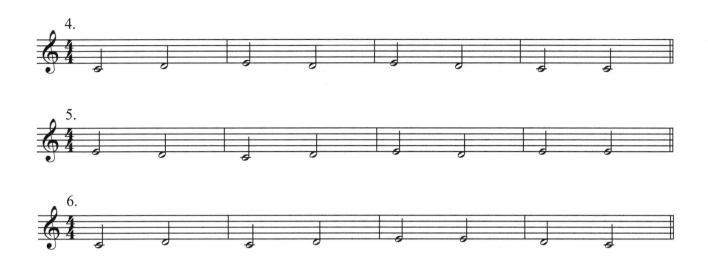

Do-Re-Mi Dictation (page 36)

Follow the Bouncing Pencil (page 37)

(Continued on next page)

Two-Step Dictation (page 38)

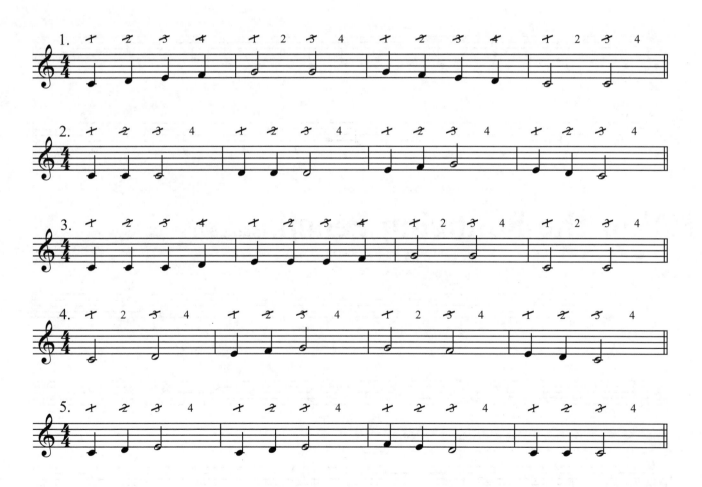